Cowboy Etiquette

Texas Bix Bender
Art by Larry Bute

GIBBS
P
SMITH

Gibbs Smith, Publisher
Salt Lake City

For Madge and all her polite critters.

First Edition
07 06 05 04 03   10 9 8 7 6 5 4 3 2 1
Text © 2003 Texas Bix Bender
Illustrations © 2003 Gibbs Smith, Publisher

Published by
Gibbs Smith, Publisher
P.O. Box 667
Layton, Utah 84041

www.gibbs-smith.com
Orders: 800.748.5439

Design by Mary Ellen Thompson, TTA Design
Printed and bound in the U.S.A.

Library of Congress Cataloging-in-Publication Data

Bender, Texas Bix, 1949-
Cowboy etiquette / by Texas Bix Bender. — 1st ed.
  p. cm.
ISBN 1-58685-241-8
1. Etiquette—Humor. 2. Cowboys—Humor. I. Title.
PN6231.E8 B46 2003
818'.5402—dc21
                              2003010846

Etiquette
is the difference
between stable manners
and table manners.

Good etiquette
starts with a smile—
unless you have something
stuck in your teeth.

At the table,
keep your
boarding house reach
in check
and don't dribble
on your boots.

Nowadays, a lot of folks
greet you with a question:
"What's up?" "How ya doin'?"
or "How's it goin'?"
The proper cowboy greeting
comes from an awareness of
where the sun is in the sky and
consists of the word "Mornin',"
"Afternoon," or "Evenin'."

Always raise the toilet seat.
And don't forget to set it
back down when you're done.
In all fairness,
cowgirls should raise it up
when they get done.
This way it's nearly always
wrong when you get there,
but good etiquette requires
everybody to be fair.

Always tip your hat
to a lady
—and they're all ladies.

If you make
a mess,
clean it up.

Spurs on the porch
are borderline.
In the house
they're over the line.

Being polite
means always being
a little nicer
than you have to be.

Never show your horse
more affection than your wife
unless you like
sleepin' in the barn.

Always try to say
the right thing first thing
after doing
the wrong thing.

Act the same way
when you don't
have company
as when you do.

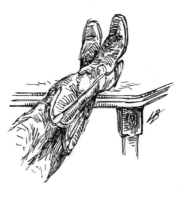

Actin' like you're big
is probably going
to have
the opposite effect.

Bragging
is
bad manners.

Good manners
go a long way
toward making
anybody more attractive.

Dumbass bumper stickers
on your pickup brand you
as the dumbass
who put them there.

Don't cut
in front and
don't crowd
from behind.

At the movies,
take off your hat, don't kick
the seat in front of you,
don't talk, and for heaven's sake
don't spit.

A man
taking a stand
on high moral grounds
just might be
standing on a bluff.

To get a conversation
off to a good start,
start off with
a compliment.

If you take something
without asking
to borrow it,
you stole it.

Nowadays some men like
to hug, slap high fives, or
bump fists when they meet.
A simple old-fashioned
handshake is still
the cowboy way.

Give up your bus seat
to a lady or elderly person—
before the bus gets
to where you're goin'.

If you open a gate, close it.
If you didn't open it,
close it anyway.

Most invitations are specific,
not open-ended.
So, it ain't polite to show up
when everybody else
is leaving and ask,
"What's for dinner?"

One sign
of good manners
is being able
to put up
with bad ones.

If you're waved off,
don't go in
without a good reason.

Don't talk
with a full mouth
or an empty head.

Knowing which fork to use
isn't nearly as important
as being good company.

When taking a herd
through a populated area,
be sure to clean up
after 'em.

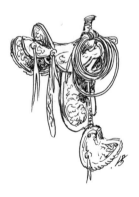

It's better to have worked
for your dinner
than to have
dressed for it.

Never start an argument
at the dinner table;
the least hungry person
always wins.

If the guests
outnumber the chairs,
it's called
a buffet.

If you've got
nothing much to say,
don't take an hour
to prove it.

If you don't know
what to talk about,
talk about three words
—and then shut up.

When you sit down,
lay your napkin in your lap.
When you get up but are
coming back, leave it in your
chair. When you're finished,
leave it on the table.

38

Don't interrupt
unless somebody's
hair is on fire.

The only good reason
to leave a party
without thanking the
host and hostess
is if you weren't invited.

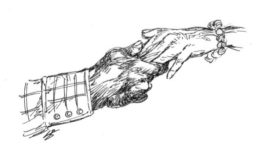

Never interfere
with another man's dog
unless the dog
is about to attach himself
to your leg.

Slurping, burping,
and gulping are only okay
when you're alone
with your dog.
Same goes for
any kind of licking.

Don't use
your napkin
to blow
your nose!

White wine is served chilled,
in a long-stemmed glass.
That's so you can hold it
by the stem and not warm
the wine with your hand.

Red wine is served at room
temperature in a short-stemmed
glass. Holding the wine by the
glass itself and
not the stem
warms the wine
and releases its
flavors.

Beer is served in a bottle,
but you can put it in a glass
if you want to.

Whiskey should never be drunk
from the bottle
unless there's no glass around
or you've already had
too much to drink.

When served escargot,
pour a little salt on it
and forget it.
It will melt while you wait
for the next course.

When you're
standing in line,
and it's a long one,
take it like a man.

If your soup is served too hot,
it's not polite
for you to blow on it.
So, ask your wife to do it.

After-dinner speeches
should be gotten
out of the way
before dinner.

When there's nothing
more to be said,
don't be saying it.

When you've invited
your in-laws over for a steak
and they show up
with a couple of cousins
you never heard of and
you only have four steaks,
cut everybody's meat for 'em.

Casual means no tie,
but get a haircut, shine your
boots, and tuck in your shirttail.
Semiformal means you'll need
a tie, a coat, and all of the above.
Black tie formal means you
probably don't wanta go.

If you're not having fish,
forget the fish fork.
Even if you are having fish,
forget the fish fork.
One fork's as good as another
unless it's in the road.

Etiquette is the art of handling
yourself, in any situation,
in a manner that doesn't
embarrass you or anyone else
and lets you keep your sense
of humor intact.

Stay home
if you're contagious.

When you meet a neighbor on
the road, always give him the
little one-finger-off-the-wheel
salute. Depending on
how you get along
with him determines
which finger you use.

Making someone
feel little
makes you
look smaller too.

Don't overload
your mouth
with opinions.

Spills and
accidents happen.
Don't make a big deal
out of 'em.

Sooner or later we all wind up sitting next to someone at dinner who is about as strange as a duck in Death Valley. Good etiquette requires  that you waddle across the desert with 'em until dessert is over.

Gossiping
is never
good etiquette.

When you're camping
on somebody else's spread,
leave without
a trace.

Don't break your arm
reaching for the check,
but don't sit
on your hands either.

Pay back
every favor.

Where people are from
and how they got here
has got nothing to do with
where they sit at the table.

Show up for dinner
clean and
respectably dressed.

Nicknames are okay
if they're not
insults.

Give age the
respect it deserves
—in people, critters,
and whiskey.

Always hold the door
for a woman—
or anyone else,
for that matter.

Women always go first
unless you're
going down stairs
or falling off a log.

It's not bad luck
to spill salt, but tossing
it over your shoulder
is a bad habit.

Don't try to pass
off your personal life
as dinner conversation.

If a woman spills her drink,
hand her a napkin
and let her do the patting.

If you make a date,
keep it.

Treat everybody
like they're
important.

Keep downwind when
approaching a cook wagon
so you don't kick up dust
on another man's plate.

Don't answer
the doorbell in
your undershorts.

Aftershave is
not a marinade.

Don't take the last piece
unless you're the last
to be served.
('Course, if you've given
everybody else a fair chance
at it, go ahead
and take the last biscuit.)

On the trail, it's all right to fork
beans right out of the can,
but never drink from the can.
It can cut your lips
and is an embarrassment
to the mules.

When sharing a can
of Vienna sausages,
it's all right
to use your fingers
to pull one out,
but taking two is rude.

When dining with nudists,
you still must wear
your bandana.

When somebody asks
you to pass 'em a biscuit,
they don't mean
overhanded.

The best year
for any wine
is the year
you drink it.

Don't serve up
family secrets
at the dinner table.

All cowboys are connoisseurs—
of horses, dogs, cattle, fences,
pickups, saddles, boots, hats,
roping, riding, belt buckles, and
rodeoing. (I ain't
including women
here because it
wouldn't be
politically correct,
and cowboys
don't know
much about 'em anyway.)

Cowboys are also
connoisseurs of cussin',
but it just ain't polite to
give public demonstrations.

Politics and religion
are hard rolls to chew on
over dinner.

Taste it
before
you salt it.

Never go anywhere
without your head
in your hat.

Good neighbors
don't need
fences.

If you have to tell
somebody you're just kiddin',
maybe yer not.

Give a good day's work
for the wage you sign on for,
and approach the work
with respect,
no matter how tedious.

A foreman should approach
a hand with respect
if he expects the hand
to show
respect for the work.

If you're the boss,
pay your hires
the best wages you can,
not the best wages you can
get away with.

Nowadays
it's okay for the woman
to ask you out
—like it was ever
up to you anyway.

At a party,
start slow
and taper off.

It's never a mistake
to offer a lady
your arm.

Remember that food
artfully arranged
has had somebody's fingers
all over it.

It's good
to know yourself—
but it's not enough.

Know-it-alls are a bother
to those of us
who really do know it all.

Never complain
—or brag—
to your date
about how much
you're spending.

A smile
is always
welcome.

When in doubt,
apologize.

Avoid frivolity
in dress
and lawsuits.

It doesn't matter
so much where you sit
as long as you
get fed.

When you're invited to dinner,
bring a little something
besides your appetite.

No
whining.

If you're on horseback
talking to someone
and they're on the ground,
dismount. It ain't polite
to talk down to people.

Taking an attitude that
everybody's out to get you
just might make everybody
want to get you.

Still the most important words
to get along in life:
Please.
Thank you.

Don't take offense
where none
was meant.

Two great stress reducers:
I'm sorry.
I forgive you.

Good manners
are like a MasterCard:
they're welcome
everywhere you go.

Tell folks
how to get on,
not where
to get off.

When you have to go,
don't tell everybody
what you're up to.
Just say "Excuse me,"
and go.

Allow others
the pleasure of
payin' you a compliment
without arguin' about it.

Allow that others
make mistakes now and then
—unless you want to be
the only one who
ever tangles his spurs.

If your job
is ridin' drag
in a roundup,
don't try to take
the point.

Keep your opinion
of yourself
to yourself.

A little
small talk
can say a lot.

Rules for a Cowboy in Wine Country

Rule #1: If the host has selected the wine, to insult the wine is to insult the host, so you like it.

Rule #2: Most wines don't need to be taken all that seriously.

Rule #3: Good wine seldom comes with a twist cap.

Rule #4. Wine lingo is not all that hard to master. If you like it, say something like, "Pardner, this dogie is a little wrinkled but stands up to the iron and smoothes out well on the palate." If you don't like it, say something like, "Amigo, this pony's legless, has the bouquet of wilted sagebrush, and goes down like yesterday's coffee."

Rule #5: If it's the only bottle of wine, it's always good.

Sooner or later we all get
our spurs tangled and trip up.
Apologize and do your best
to make it right.
That's all you can do.

Don't take your boots
off under the table.
You don't want to compete
with the bouquet
of the wine.

Eating with your fingers
is okay if there are no forks,
spoons, or knives around.
But eating with someone
else's fingers is almost
never good etiquette.

It's okay to let
yourself go sometimes.
Just be sure you can
let yourself back in.

Farts
are not considered
good dinner conversation.

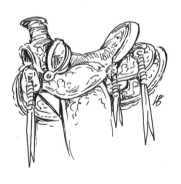